PILING BLOOD

ALSO BY AL PURDY

The Enchanted Echo 1944
Pressed on Sand 1955
Emu, Remember 1956
The Crafte So Longe to Lerne 1959
Poems for All the Annettes 1962
The Blur In Between 1963
The Cariboo Horses 1965
North of Summer: Poems from Baffin Island 1968
Poems for All the Annettes: Selected Poems to 1965 1968
The Quest for Ouzo 1969
Love in a Burning Building 1970
Selected Poems 1972
Sex & Death 1973
In Search of Owen Roblin 1974
Hiroshima Poems 1972
On the Bearpaw Sea 1973
Sundance at Dusk 1976
The Poems of Al Purdy 1976
At Marsport Drugstore 1977
A Handful of Earth 1977
No Second Spring 1978
Moths in the Iron Curtain 1978
Being Alive: Poems 1958–1978 1978
The Stone Bird 1981
Bursting into Song . . . An Al Purdy Omnibus 1982
Birdwatching at the Equator 1983

PROSE

No Other Country 1977
The Bukowski/Purdy Letters, 1964–1974 1984
Morning and It's Summer 1984

AS EDITOR

The New Romans: Candid Canadian Opinions of the U.S. 1968
Fifteen Winds 1969
Storm Warning 1971
Storm Warning 2 1976

Al Purdy

PILING BLOOD

McCLELLAND AND STEWART

The Canadian Publishers
McClelland and Stewart Limited
25 Hollinger Road, Toronto M4B 3G2

Canadian Cataloguing in Publication Data

Purdy, Al, 1918–
Piling blood

Poems.
ISBN 0-7710-7213-9

I. Title.

PS8531.U73P55 1984 C811'.54 C84-099148-7
PR9199.3.P87P55 1984

The publisher makes grateful acknowledgment to the Ontario Arts Council and the Canada Council for their assistance.

Set in Kennerley by The Typeworks, Vancouver
Printed and bound in Canada by Gagné Ltd.

To the memory of Peter Dwyer

ON THE PLANET EARTH

She was lovely as sunrise
meeting sunset at the world's edge
without a chaperone and blushing

I mentioned this to her
mentioned also Jungian theory
of the unconscious
                                        I said
"All your life there will be
visitors in your mind
you don't know about
and I'm there too
when for no apparent
reason you blush
that's me kid – "

PILING BLOOD

PILING BLOOD

It was powdered blood
in heavy brown paper bags
supposed to be strong enough
to prevent the stuff from escaping
but didn't

We piled it ten feet high
right to the shed roof
working at Arrow Transfer
on Granville Island
The bags weighed 75 pounds
and you had to stand on two
of the bags to pile the top rows
I was six feet three inches
and needed all of it

I forgot to say
the blood was cattle blood
horses sheep and cows
to be used for fertilizer
the foreman said

It was a matter of some delicacy
to plop the bags down softly
as if you were piling dynamite
if you weren't gentle
the stuff would belly out
from bags in brown clouds
settle on your sweating face
cover hands and arms
enter ears and nose
seep inside pants and shirt
reverting back to liquid blood
and you looked like

you'd been scalped
by a tribe of
particularly unfriendly
Indians and forgot to die

We piled glass as well
it came in wooden crates
two of us hoicking them
off trucks into warehouses
every crate
weighing 200 pounds
By late afternoon
my muscles would twitch and throb
in a death-like rhythm
from hundreds of bags of blood
and hundreds of crates of glass

Then at Burns' slaughterhouse
on East Hastings Street
I got a job part time
shouldering sides of frozen beef
hoisting it from steel hooks
staggering to and from
the refrigerated trucks
and eerie freezing rooms
with breath a white vapour
among the dangling corpses
and the sound of bawling animals
screeched down from an upper floor
with their throats cut
and blood gurgling into special drains
for later retrieval

And the blood smell clung to me
clung to clothes and body
sickly and sweet
and I heard the screams
of dying cattle

and I wrote no poems
there were no poems
to exclude the screams
which boarded the streetcar
and travelled with me
till I reached home
turned on the record player
and faintly
in the last century
heard Beethoven weeping

FUNERAL

The preacher called beforehand
to make sure God
occupied a place in my heart
or somewhere nearby
I made a mistake
told him the truth
said I wasn't religious
During the funeral chapel sermon
called a eulogy by some
among my mother's friends and relatives
dressed in their black Sunday best
and the smell of sweat and formaldehyde
he preached the evil of unbelievers
clubbed me with clichés
stunned me with Job and Jeremiah
and the sheer surprise of it
pinned me to the chair
The United Church minister
kept hammering away
knowing I was a prisoner
and couldn't escape
because a son must be there
because a son must bear witness
when half his reason for being
vanishes into the earth
and there is no longer
a warm presence behind him
he stands naked
on the needle point of now
before the rushing winds of time

At first it was exhilarating
being so damn furious
drunk and sober simultaneously

atheism seemed glorious
then changed my mind
wanted to be a believer
in order to render aid
and comfort to Satan
Finally some relief
that it took a phony god
to make this bastard possible
then amusement that my immortal soul
was worth only twenty minutes
as the red-faced prick thundered on
for his audience of one
and the dead woman listening

THINGS OF SOME IMPORTANCE

My wife and I were travelling
on the plane back from Madrid
when this girl with long red
hair down to her waist
stopped at my seat to
let the booze buggy pass
I said "Beautiful hair"
She said "Thank you kind sir"
I said "Don't you think so?"
She said "So many other
people have told me the same
thing I can't disagree"
Perfect answer
neither modest nor conceited
a girl of obvious character
and we smiled about it
just before she proceeded
I thought the incident trivial
but things of some importance
faded grey in that red glory and
my priorities kept shifting
into high from neutral
and another self an alter
– ego I'd hardly even spoken
to on previous occasions
intruded on my reverie and
they waltzed away together
when we landed in New York
and after clearing Customs
we went shopping for the baby

MENELAUS AND HELEN

Was this the face that launched a thousand ships,
And burned the topless towers of Ilium?
Christopher Marlowe

Menelaus, the Bear, King of Sparta,
homeward bound with Helen, his runaway wife,
after the death of Priam's fifty sons
– only Aeneas of all the Trojan princelings
surviving the slaughter. Troy running blood,
the marketplace a horror, the people slaves
– beyond the last screams of dying men,
birdsong – at the far limits of both sounds,
meeting at the edges, high notes and low notes,
water over mossy stones, velvet scraping iron.
Menelaus, the Bear, his ships blown south
by Poseidon's wind, oars broken, men discouraged,
three galleys dismasted, the gods unheeding,
beached for a month on a limestone island near Egypt,
where seals slithered like wet black slugs,
making seal sounds of human melancholy –

At Sparta:
to be a king with servants and advisors bowing
and scraping, some of them too nervous to speak,
then meet a woman and yourself be humbled and speechless –
when I first saw Helen it was some time
before I could again breathe naturally.
Even manslayer Achilles was troubled.
I noticed he held his breath for several
seconds in the same air she breathed,
before it occurred to him to think of death
again, and chariots were guttural in his throat.
I couldn't wait to get her into bed.
But it was disappointing, nothing worked out;

she didn't smile at me, she grinned,
as if I'd been boasting about my manhood,
and been caught short. I almost blushed.
But a king must king it. My body servant,
for instance, kept falling asleep
and forgetting to polish my armour,
or wipe gravy stains from the tunic.
Grooms need watching, herdsmen are careless
with all that half-wild flesh they tend.
Entranced by Helen, I hardly noticed.
Then – discipline must be maintained, I said,
and flogged them. I will not say
that I grew tired of Helen, but those blue eyes
in which you think to see the sea and see
emptiness, discontent, see the receding
tides of love, deep slumber of the gods –
Besides, she nagged me. Not with words,
just that blue gaze, an azure stillness,
like the sound you hear inside your ears,
before sleep: I was trapped in deafening stillness.
As for Paris? How could I blame Paris?
Of course I said I did, the mandatory
wronged husband's predictable reaction.
No doubt I did look slightly ridiculous,
and Agamemnon, my dear brother, kept saying that:
Menelaus, he said, I think you enjoy it,
I think you enjoy being made a fool.
That did annoy me. And I could see the snickers
twitch on all the faces but Odysseus' face.
Paris: well, she was bathing when he saw her,
and naked her sex blazed like a sunset.
The grin she had for me, visible in darkness,
no doubt became a daylight smile for Paris.
And that Trojan story that nothing at all happened,
whoever tells it chortles inside their soul.
All the sun-leagues to Troy on open decks
of Paris' pleasure-galley: they fucked.
Or, if you will, made love, they merged the words,

fuck-love, love-fuck: the gods alone
can make distinction between those activities,
one physical and employing the excretory
orifices, the other mystical as miracles.
The lovers, bewitched in a green sea-garden,
so young all birthdays were tomorrow;
the old steersman watching, his scrawny body
reflected in water, a scarecrow for fish.
At any rate, my thoughts of Helen changed.
When Troy burned, and we cut the throats
of anyone who looked at us sideways,
I saw the flames mingle with blue in her eyes,
I saw the eager blue run to join crimson.
She stood aloof, with Paris dead somewhere,
his face hacked into a red horror,
she savouring it, enjoying it, as Achilles did
when dragging Hector's body round the walls.
She was goddess then, death and life,
the power bestowing both. I shivered.
Twenty days. I tell you, twenty days
we stopped on that limestone island,
while seals oinked at us. She complained.
She said Paris wouldn't have permitted this.
She said, kill the seals. I saw red flames
from tall Troy towers and mud-brick houses
flicker in her blue eyes. I hate blue eyes.
What colour are Aphrodite's eyes? Blue?
We slaughtered a few seals to please Helen.
I asked an old man what island this was.
There was trouble with the barbarous language
these Egyptians speak. I thought he said Pharos.
Later I was told it was Pharaoh's island,
and Pharaoh is the king of that country.
I would have asked his pleasure and his aid
as one king to another if I had known.
Wind abated, the sea calmed, we hoped
Poseidon had his mind on something else. And sailed.
Home in Sparta, the grooms were still lazy,

my servants were half-asleep in daytime,
thieves made off with twenty head of horses.
We caught them next day; I cut their throats.
Helen looked bored. Nothing had changed.
I kept hearing tales of mermaids on Pharos,
and talk of Proteus, the shape-changer,
who does quickly what men do slowly.
Some said I'd asked him for sailing directions,
and forced an answer. Briefly, all was heroic,
Helen a goddess, poets dreamed their nonsense,
ten years under Trojan walls an instant.
I said the mermaids were seals, Helen human.
Nobody listens. I see the young gardener's gaze
on Helen; his breath stutters and catches; her maid,
dressing her, is almost afraid to touch her.
She is 58 years old, and forgets my name;
she dyes her hair yellow. Her eyes are faded;
shortsighted, she sees me as a vague blur,
complains unendingly of bedroom dampness,
totters the parapets to bother my guardsmen
with questions of when the Greeks will rescue her.

Gods, Gods, you have taken my youth for this,
leaving the memory of roaring Agamemnon,
replicas of Odysseus and myself, bursting into Troy
from the belly of a child's plaything,
the children who were us, and murdered Troy.
It keeps happening:
The burning towers of Troy; Helen's faded eyes;
blurred sights she saw along those walls;
the far-heard cries, a windy roar of chariot wheels;
her complaints: "I can't sleep for all the racket."
And this obscures whatever reality is:
seals changing into mermaids, and Helen
slowly into a caricature of a goddess;
myself with hand that trembles on my sword,
an old man the servants ridicule

behind his back. It is all a kind of sleep:
shadows grow to substance, an old fence post
becomes a crouching warrior, some berry bushes
a distant army on which the helmets glisten –
and no one comes this morning with my breakfast.

VOLTAIRE

Travelling home to Circy
with Madame du Châtelet
over the frozen roads of Europe
at night in March 1737:
a wheel came off the carriage
on Voltaire's side and it turned over
piling everything – baggage
the "divine Emilie" and her maid
atop Voltaire with considerable
objection from the great man
At the same time two servants
driving the carriage also fell
and horses haunted by ghosts of predators
stampeded inside their harness
When Voltaire was extricated
and servants worked to restore order
quieting the nervous horses
he began to enjoy himself
Cushions were laid on the winter road
Voltaire and his mistress sat on them
laughing together about the accident
until the carriage was repaired
and appreciating the night sky
One of the servants describes it:
"Not a tree, not a house
disturbed the expanse of the horizon.
M. de Voltaire and Madame
du Châtelet were in ecstasies:
wrapped in furs, they discussed
the nature and orbits of the stars
and their destination in space
while their teeth chattered.
If only they had had a telescope,
their joy would have been complete."

All over Europe
generals marched their armies
the Inquisition tortured heretics
kings sat uneasily on their thrones
sniffing their wine suspiciously
and babies were waiting to be born
while "divine Emilie" and her lover
laughed on the frozen roads of France
Their moment of delight returns
again to us in books
and the memory of very old men
who were babies long ago
the words travel like fireflies
in starlight & sunlight & moonlight
and twinkle from their graves

LOST IN THE BADLANDS

We walk into a wound
a torn gash in the earth
where soft fingers of water
grew claws and raged at stone

Of course we have no business
being here at all
in the grim badlands above the Red
Deer River's flood plain
(a big sign where we entered said NO
TRESPASSING UNLESS ACCOMPANIED BY GUIDE)
walking for exercise at 5:30 P.M.
(or amusement and to fend off boredom)
into these immense vistas of time
toward the Upper Cretaceous Period
seventy-five million years ago
locked away from the high flickering
blue sky by two stone walls
a canyon leading downward
into the dinosaurs' graveyard
where a movement or an action
begun in the past
is never completed
but continues now
in nerves of my trembling fingers

No vegetation here
but higher on the walls wispy grasses
cling to rust-coloured sandstone
No wind or sound of voices
only this non-silence
a mirage of screaming sound
or an illusion of silence
as if every animal that ever lived

and died was struggling
trying to get your attention
and all the calcium carbonate
in your bones shuffling
its components uneasily

The books tell you something
with names to grasp at nothing
geology zoology palaeontology
and every metre of strata
above me means a million years
but this dinosaur graveyard
400 feet below flat prairie
has no reality in books
– the mirage screaming is omitted
by a typesetting machine
Some learned apeman
with academic degrees
from a dozen universities
overloads your own primitive
computer with excess information
about continental plates
and the Great Death
at the end of the Cretaceous
when three-quarters of all life
on earth died swiftly or slowly
in fact everything larger
than 20 pounds or so
including dinosaurs
– the academic with the degrees
that man didn't feel a thing
in fact left something out
about how the sun went down at 5:30
P.M. one evening and next morning
the Great Dying began
until nothing of any size remained
but some scampering rodents
a few half-assed mammals

still trying to say something
back there at the end of the Cretaceous

I grab at shaley walls ineffectually
trying to keep my difficult balance
touching a coal seam inches thick
(a compressed ten thousand years?
– of peat swamps)
with furred or scaled forepaws
while my wife with amazon stride
forges businesslike into the past
I try to glimpse in all this shadowy
chronology a narrow band of iridium
in earth strata: placed there
sixty-five million years ago
when an asteroid six miles wide
exploded onto the earth
and smothering dust circled in the sky
killing flora and fauna
with a cloudy fist

All these presumed facts
are in fact only presumed
amount to an immense puzzle
about animal origins
in which I can lose myself
and seem to listen mindlessly
hear dozens of volcanos
exploding west of here
see the sky black with ashes
no sunlight seeps through
becoming vaguely aware
that one of the fossil animals
is saying something to me
my wife yelling at my ear
"Let's get outa here
climb up into the sunlight"
I resist this move conservatively
expecting to lose the argument

and we climb 50 feet or so
– into a dull grey land
of eroded chalky hills
like Satan's nightmare
into another time of being:
thinking of the great lizards
living near the Bearpaw Sea
stretching from the arctic
to the present Gulf of Mexico
and how we're crossing and re-crossing
the paths of tyrannosaurs
and pterodactyls occupying
the same space they occupied
my body coinciding with theirs
knowing those giant heartbeats
knocking on empty air
living so near to them
that a snap of the fingers
or twist of perspective
would make them visible
clomping bone corridors
joining my thoughts of them
their image taking over
the pictures in my brain
In fact they *are* visible
an aperture in my primitive brain
allows their enormous heads
to peer into the mammal mind
with red reptilian mouths

Westward the red sun
dips on a ragged horizon
and clock time emerges
from the shadowy limbic brain
awareness of gathering darkness
causing definite uneasiness
I yammer in my wife's ear
"How in hell we gonna get outa here?
– it's a hall of mirrors

everything looks the same"
She gives me a look
one of those looks you expect
when she thinks you're silly
"If we get lost in this place
we're gonna stay all night
It's damn near night right now
and past the tourist season
nobody even knows we're here
All the park guides are cuddling
their girl friends in Calgary"
(I wonder if every female dinosaur
ate her husband and therefore
the species became extinct?)
We scramble round buttes and hoodoos
my wife leading the way
and me following meekly fearful
in this grey land of lost time
where everything that ever happened
is eerily still happening
every death and every birth
And that red sun tucked into bed
under the horizon is certainly
the same star that sank west of
the Bearpaw Sea in crimson and gold
In all this maze of conjecture
I mean the simultaneity of things
not the false measurement of clocks
but the instant of the dinosaurs
whose instant I am part of
exploding suns and plunging asteroids
iridium jargon and geologic nonsense
which vanish as the brute face
of man lifts cunning from a ledge
of sandstone to sing inside my bones

Emerging from the past
we reach the dangerous present
a dirt track of tourist road:

a studied lack of expression
on my wife's face as she proceeds
to ignore the frightened stranger
at her side a while longer
to prevent conjugal warfare
as we return slowly together
into the wilds of intimacy

IN THE BEGINNING WAS THE WORD

In the Beginning was not *the Word*
– but a Chirrup.
D. H. Lawrence

We made our speech from moving water
a sound that seems to ache
when there is no pain
whispering faintly in the heart's darkness
– and listening at still pools in the forest
we saw the strangers and fled in fear
from their floating faces
We made our speech from the wind's voice
singing to earth when the moon sleeps
and in weariness after hunting
the red throat of fire the white tongues of rain
We made it from the sound of food
on little pattering feet running
with terrified eyes in the forest
while we watched in ambush
with wet mouths
We made our speech from all things
weaker than us and the sounds moved
when our tongues moved
as if they were alive and they were alive
and our children played with the sounds
until they remembered silence

We made our speech from the beast's growl
the bird's chirp and dumb thunder muttering
and from the ice-spirit at the glacier's edge
desolate voices of the lost ones calling
And we changed the colours of things
into sounds of themselves

for we were the great imitators
and we spoke the strong words that invented men
and became ourselves
And we painted our dead crimson
in order that the blood should remember
in all their voyaging the place they came from

And after the essence of everything
had exchanged itself for words and became
another being and could even be summoned
from far distance we chanted a spell of names
and we said "Mountain be our friend"
and we said "River guard us from enemies"
And we said what it seemed the gods themselves
might say if we had dreamed them and they
had dreamed us from their high places
and they spoke to us in the forest
from the river and the mountain
and the mouths of the ochre-painted dead
had speech again and the waters
spoke and the silence had words

And our children remembered –

SEAL PEOPLE

The big boss bull *harrumphs*
disapproving ten feet from shore
adolescents are darker
drops of moon-water
enclosed in bright sun-water
make little enthusiastic *oinks*
at the tourist visitors
lolloping back and forth
wild with joy
churning the Humboldt Current to froth
One whiskery juvenile is curious about me
snuffs at my extended hand
wants to know
why I can't join the fun
For a moment
I feel an electric jolt
of adult tenderness
as if the inside organs
of my own body had emerged
and were living separately from me
making hoarse little *oink* sounds
– my lungs float in tropic seas
liver a dark shadow remembering water
and the difficult amphibian drag-race
across forgotten sands
kidneys and heart
bob in the salt sea
and I croon some primitive song
while they call me to join them

When it's time to go
I have not retrieved all of myself
and may never

Galapagos Islands

IGUANA

Hunkered on hands and knees
then collapsing sideways
cheek on stony ground
in order to see close-up:
Tyrannosaurus thirty feet high
looming over my head
about to have me for breakfast
My left eye sees separately
seventy million years in the past
but the right eye sees only
a harmless vegetarian
this spring day in 1980
He regards me benevolently
in fact reminds of my Uncle Wilfred
who chewed plug tobacco
and while reading Tennyson
never missed the spittoon
from a distance of at least
fifty years ago

I am travelling of course in time
expect to encounter relations
maybe a mislaid cousin
I didn't like much anyway
across the lava peninsulas
indentured to Polyphemus
maybe a long-dead brother
I wanted to say goodbye to
or kooky aunts and uncles
and clutch my craziness tightly
for fear I might grow sane

However
back near Darwin Station
the black iguanas gather

and they're actually domestic
a trois or dix ménage
the big one old man God
who bullies his female harem
some basic law of the flesh
requires that he demonstrate
requires in the act of creation
that he demonstrate lizard restraint
A separate species
at evolution's stop-light
silent and unaware
that in Mexico for instance
they're regarded as tasty as chicken
here old man God is a sultan
before man a reptile Jehovah
and before Jehovah – what?

With a modicum of trepidation
I touch his back with my foot
expecting iguana explosions
thunder at Darwin Station
at least the earth to open
and my flesh crawls with the effort
But God just sways his head
sways it up and down up down
irritated at this presumption
What can I be but humble
for the reptile and mammal primate
may never touch each other
without fear of opposites
and I feel sad
knowing I will never understand him
nor the races before and after
the star ship's rocket landing
understand nothing but now
balanced in the needle's eye
and the impulse to touch God
is as close as I'll ever come

Galapagos Islands

ADAM AND NO EVE

His name is *Geochelone (elephantopus) abingdoni*
a giant yellow-faced tortoise
the last of his species
(call him Lonesome George)
from Abingdon Island
now coddled and cuddled by keepers
the nursemaid scientists
of Darwin Research Station

They have posted reward money
these scientists
ten thousand dollars
for just one female
of Lonesome George's species
but no female has ever been found
Lonesome George's relatives
brothers and sisters and cousins
stern great aunts and harrumphing uncles
are gone from Abingdon Island
and the world

(Summon the bounty hunters:
is there movement somewhere
among the man-high cactus
with four legs instead of two
and neck like a periscope
wandering the 20th century?
– a clumsy shadow blunders
through laboratory glassware
could that be Great Aunt Martha?
– a sudden splash of light
along the mangrove shoreline
could that be Abingdon Annie?)

Man with his symbol-making brain
has said ten thousand dollars

equals one female
but there are millions and billions
of dollars in pockets and banks
and no tortoises in their vaults
or human pockets and wallets
– in fact make it a billion
dollars for one nubile female
the result is exactly the same

Not again shall mud conceive
or the stars bear witness
and lightning flash over chaos
nor any deity of the flesh
send his small amphibians
scuttling onto land for safety
the amino acids are dissolved
their formulas forgotten
– and whatever love may be
weighed and counted and measured
in books and artistic symbols
one female tortoise (shaped
somewhat like an old shoe)
has taken it with her alone
into the darkness

Galapagos Islands

BIRDS AND BEASTS

On the road to Ameliasburg
whip-poor-wills from nearby woods
sing the very first thought they had
when they first came out of the egg
surprised at being alive
and killdeers run in charcoal dusk
with sparks from the sun's bonfire
while the great black robes of night
slowly lower and lower
Running in front of the car
swerve swerve go little feet
scoot scoot from carbon breath
and roar roar of the Ford beast
home to your nest

Re the whip-poor-will:
rumour has it and I would agree
the song actually resembles "More Still"
in the sense of discreet music criticism
instead of the traditional "Poor Will"
whoever that fellow was anyway
i.e. not at all iambic or trochaic
it is like some most enjoyable grief
like the first tears I never let fall
for the first woman I ever loved
when she went away

Poor Newfoundland poor B.C. and Alberta
they do not go there
mourn ye rugged Newfoundlanders and Albertans
and mourn ye bereft westcoasters likewise
who never hear the bonfire song
the dusk song the heart song of home
And verily be complacent ye effete easterners

for whom the jewelled guts resound
and pour their sorcery in our ears
jug-jug for dirty ears

Nearby they cry "Sleep Well Sleep Well"
to brothers in the woods
and these reply "We Will We Will"
while the little red bonfire dies
and silence   silence falls

HOW IT FEELS TO BE OLD

I

Visiting the old house in Trenton
where I was a child forever
– shit-coloured varnished floors
(my actual opinion of them then)
light bulbs dangling like hanged men
jail cell closets
that omnipresent odour
of mothballs and urine
me the prisoner inside a child's body
– if one could conceive
of all small journeys made
between bathroom bedroom and kitchen
inside this grim circumference
of mammal matrix
conceive them as indelible white trails
the spoor of time
those multiple trails transformed
into a large ball of white
yarn my mother's knitting
needle eyes ignored?

Conceive of time
in which all actions float
like drowned bodies on a river
unsinkable in time
And childhood
in which my chicken-killing dog
was about to be executed for his crimes
and was beginning to suspect
and his eyes his eyes
I find myself staring fixedly
at a knot in the wooden stairway
of the old house through which

a frowsy airedale dog is peering
and I have no word of comfort
for him – only a sigh
when that moment ends
and this one begins

2

In old age he slept
on the Mowat doorstep
near Quinte Bay
and kept farting
waking sometimes to snap
at flies and miss often
visiting female dogs
failed to disturb his reverie

Elmer was ancient
for a dog – nearly fifteen
a black and white spaniel
with long floppy ears
and that look of passionate meditation
in reaching the last extremity
preachers have on the toilet seat

Sirius swung on a black
cobweb overhead
cows mooed discontent
and far-distant younger dogs
berated the moon
when Elmer embarked on Quinte
He swam straight outward
toward a dark shore
several miles away
Angus missed him
and rowed after him
called to him coaxingly

helped him into the boat
He was dead next morning

At the hour of departure
there seems to me little
difference between species
and that's as good a way
to leave as any
(Dylan notwithstanding):
swim straight outward
toward a distant shore
with the dog star overhead
and music on the waters

A TYPICAL DAY IN WINNIPEG

My car has a dead battery
on accounta I left the headlights
on in a parking lot
I look around at all the damn snow
provided wholesale for my discomfort
then start walking down the frozen
road in search of a tow
truck: – no use hitch-hiking
there's very little traffic besides
Winnipeggers hate pedestrians
especially when it's 20 below
I take a shortcut across a field
which will save me maybe a mile
– snow is shallow near the road
but farther in the stuff is deep
underneath no doubt
rabbits with Quebec heaters
worms wearing parkas
My feet plunge like a spavined horse
until I'm up to my ass
in snow and wheezing badly
knowing a diet of junk food and beer
has unfitted me for athletic endeavours
I pause to seriously consider
a choice of en avant or backwards
then plough another ten feet panting
thinking: this white stuff is beauty
if you got that kinda mind
which I ain't – beauty is shit
here exemplified and made manifest
The shit-snow is up past my navel
and that's kinda alarming
since my navel is higher than most
It occurs to me I could just sit here

and await rescue by helicopter
or maybe a student from Manitoba U.
could arrive with a dogsled
It also occurs to me that death
would be easy in this situation
which seems quite ludicrous
like drowning in a bathtub
I'm half a mile from the road
snow deep deeper and deepest
(Winnipeggers found frozen every spring
clutching Hawaiian travel folders)
At my age I have no pride
any more about backing out of
a fight or not taking a dare and
rejecting other things of like nature
I turn around to go back
with beauty up to my chest by now
wheezing and coughing
tongue stuck to the roof of
my mouth like a shred of dry leather
my left foot reaching with
difficulty and passing my right
foot and vice-versa
in panicky weakness
Well obviously the road is reached again
I revert to the trivial
and there's nobody to complain to
but I complain just the same
start toward that service station
which someone has likely moved
farther away just to annoy me
grumbling softly to myself in transit
shit-snow   shit-beauty   shit-city
thinking of that dead battery
burnt toast for breakfast this morning
and the wife who wouldn't come
west with me to Winnipeg
because she said I needed to

live alone this ice-age winter
on accounta my bed temper whereas
I am renowned for personal
sweetness which I resolve to
curb and arrive at the service
station fairly unfrozen feeling
somehow ennobled and ready to
argue with the mechanic

VANCOUVER

A state of mind of course this city
some geographic quirk
can sparkle in the sauntering eye
or glimmer grey in sullen heart
reflect the moods of trees
– on certain mornings of such clarity
mountains are seen to have moved
stumped on stone legs to Granville Street
– at the traffic light's first green
rose-red spring salmon migrate
the intersection at Hastings & Main

There have been Kitsilano sunsets
that dodge around the glum hotels
a huge red ten-dimensional face
hangs from the horizon's picture
window and never does descend
                                        Surprise Surprise
for every tourist corner turned
discover other suns come trundling
from planetary cradles to join
them at the sea's doorway
and finally merge
in one gigantic rose suspended
from a clock tower in the sky

Less lyrical the fog
– mooing tormented voices
of ships whispering in from the Gulf
at Coal Harbour fishing boats
mutter together in the tide slop
There is a lostness even inside buildings
secretaries peer from office windows
wanting to be safe with their lovers

pedestrians walk with hands outstretched
colour-blind in a kind of sleep
in an invasion of the grey flowers
and after a week or ten days of it
the world becomes Biblical
the god of sextant and astrolabe
haunts ships in the harbour

City of the great trees
metropolis of sawdust
and blackberries growing wild
a million black suns
at False Creek mouth
City at the continent's edge
where everyone was born three
hours younger than the grey east
and sometimes light is so luminescent
the air glows glows internally
and nobody breathes for a moment
City of mountains and sea
I have changed much
in my viewpoints and intolerant attitudes
but some things are unchanging
they deserve your love
the fog and the sea and the mountains
the streets of summer

"THE ELEPHANT IS SLOW TO MATE – "?

D. H. Lawrence

Not so at "Lion Safari" near Palm Beach
several tons of grey-mud-coloured jumbo
with six-foot dong rear to glum sky
rejoicing thereat greatly and –
The same basic instinct
impelled Paris & Helen and Hero & Leander
(not to mention classical romance)
Still and all hard to imagine
Leander Jumbo dog-paddling the Hellespont
threshing between Europe and Asia nightly
fish nibbling his luminous dong
Hero Jumbo waving her trunk for guidance
Aphrodite's temple in elephant uproar

Two ostriches
also in amatory mood
Tristram Ostrich with "the whole science
of venerie at his fingertips" (read wingtips?)
tho neither lover dies from feathery encounter
Iseult Ostrich is undeniably perturbed
Beauty resides no doubt in beholder's optics
and it's instructive for us higher orders
of creation to witness barnyard basics
realize anew romance ends with copulation
the excretory orifice (as Yeats would have it)
a site of enemas and noisome exhalations

My dear my sweet my purest love
lest eye or ear offend thee with supersonic
anal music: our affection keep platonic
read Marvell with loathing and virtue
thus safeguarded by menopause and plumbing

chant we two in unison our slogan for the future
fucking briefly is for animals
and talking about it forever only human
et cetera

NAMES

For George Galt

Birthing, begetting and dying
– the great hammers of being,
each one thudding against the skull,
each one obliterating the others –

When it was nearly time to die,
Marcus Flavinius, Centurion of
the Second Cohort, Augusta Legion,
by letter to his cousin, Tertullus,
in Rome, concerning rumours of sellouts,
plots, moneygrubbing, treason there:
"When we left our native soil, Tertullus,
we were told we were going to defend
the sacred rights of the empire and
of the people to whom we bring our
protection and civilization. Please tell
me the rumours I hear of this treachery
at home are not true – " Nevertheless,
observed in the bright glare of history,
the rumours were entirely accurate.

When it was nearly time to die,
Oberleutnant Conrad Schmidt, minor
cog in General Erwin Rommel's Afrika
Korps, dying of shrapnel wounds somewhere
between the Quattara Depression and
a little railway station in the Western
Desert called El Alamein – watching blood
drip from his chest in time with the second
hand of his watch onto dirty gravel,
measuring his remaining life by
its quickly decreasing volume:
remembering

persistent rumours of Jewish death camps,
remembering
a dead friend's opinion that Hitler
was a psychotic monster,
and wondering if he, Conrad Schmidt,
his last years spent in the Panzerarmie,
had wasted his life.

How not to waste your life?
– no reliable information available.
One could mention, in passing:
even the last act of death
provides only a few hints.
Earlier, during that mid-life period
when the senses overwhelm the mind,
and the calendar blossoms days,
and nothing has much urgency,
questions about personal integrity
are often regarded as trivial.
It seems to me these particular names
are synonymous with the question itself,
and remember their names:
Marcus Flavinius, Centurion
of the Augusta Legion;
Conrad Schmidt, Oberleutnant
in the Afrika Korps:
two men about to die,
who spent their last few moments
wondering how they could change things
on the earth they were leaving –

THERE IS OF COURSE A LEGEND

Domenico Theotocopoulos
in the stained glass shroud of Toledo
dead 370 years –

After dinner a few drinks then bed
in lodgings at the tourist parador
a hotel built where El Greco painted
his vision of Toledo
from high hills above the city
I sleep and wake – wake and sleep
a mosquito buzzing at my ears
completely ignores my wife
in its quest for rich red blood
Around 3 A.M. I've had enough
struggle into my pants
and escort that mosquito ceremoniously
to the door – it waits for me
with old-world courtesy
at the stairway singing
Toreador
We sneak past the sleepy desk clerk
opening the outside door softly
enter a blasted landscape of stone
rubble and scrub bushes in the high
hills above Toledo
Without surprise
I see El Greco hunched on the rocks
his brush moving in long sweeps of colour
painting his loved city
My mosquito buzzes uncertainly
inside its different continuum
I gesture toward the artist
"Go get him boy"
(thus betraying ignorance of gender)

My mosquito indicates gratitude
with a little flirt of wings
and dives to attack:
"Geronimo Domenico!"
and seems puzzled to find nothing there
But El Greco decidedly *is there*
wrapped in an old blanket
and scarf from Dona Jeronima
("Domenico it's cold in the high hills
– if you will insist on wandering
off in the middle of the night
with these crazy ideas of yours
you must dress for it – ")
Her expression behind dark eyes
is a brightening tenderness
matching his own – this 16th
century outlandish Greek from a far
island beyond her imagining
who touched something inside her
Looking over El Greco's shoulder
at roiled clouds breaking reforming
and light behind them
and a lost moon somewhere
there's a near correspondence
between the light in Dona Jeronima's
eyes and the painted light
above the darkened city of Toledo
a reality outside of time
tenderness preserved in paint
Looking from one to the other
the painted and the actual city
tile-roofed buildings drained of colour
windows blind eyes watching
in the bone-grey night
only an artitist's brush moving
in a dream its hairy finger
across the sleep of animals and men
supplies a human meaning

Colder on the mountain
a few drops of rain
El Greco wraps the old blanket
and Dona Jeronima's scarf closer
silver veins of lightning cross the sky
the land gasps for breath
no rain for a very long time
and despite Cardinal Nino de Guevara
and his Inquisition thumb screws
nothing is either possible or provable
except El Greco's painting
which he gathers along with brushes
and colours in little wooden boxes
and starts off down the mountain
a little middle-aged balding man
the Greek refugee from Crete
pupil of Titian and Tintoretto
rejected in Venice and Rome
rejected by Philip II rejected
by everyone except Dona Jeronima
who thinks him a genius
and he probably is
stumbling down the dark hills
above Toledo thinking of the light
light like sky silver
that gleamed a moment in Dona Jeronima
and echoed itself in the painting
an old man going home
followed by a baffled mosquito

I return to the parador bedroom
ready for sleep
my wife still asleep – then I too
for 370 years and more
until death awakens me

Toledo, Spain

ON THE INTELLIGENCE OF WOMEN

(Of whom the only example I have
near at hand is my wife)

She can figure out exactly
who the television villain is
unravelling complexities of melodrama
with a kind of female trigonometry
Now that's trivial
as also the ability to unravel
various subterranean human motives may be
(Whereas I act by impatient instinct
which has to do with nuance and behaviour
the way past actions have marked a face
as well as who gains what for which)
She arrives quickly at a problem's heart
touches a spot some delicate place
physical or abstract in cerebral
hyperspace and the thing plainly explodes
I regard this as quite miraculous
as also the gyrocompass in her head
which places the universe in relation
to our bargain basement box spring
Listening for it sometimes when she's asleep
I hear a little whirring sound
that might be just breathing the normal noise
an uncommon person makes not a deployment
of enormous forces electron and proton etc.
or adjustment of Archimedes' lever
for a ritual burning of the breakfast toast
As for deity she regards anyone
more godlike than me as male chauvinist
Yes I know it all sounds trivial
but to be lost somewhere in the Mexican desert
or atop buttes and hoodoos in Alberta badlands

where everything is so different it's the same
and have her say casually "This way dear"
and be so unvariably right it's unarguable
which I invariably do just to keep in practice
– now that's mysterious
She remembers anything relevant to money
has directional antennae for the stuff
in city streets or stores with bargains
she bought two years ago last August
and how it rained that day at three o'clock
Curiously she can't remember last week last month
last year and very little of her childhood
which she claims is blocked out because unpleasant
Whereas my own memory ranges the entire gamut
of everything I've experienced or can conceive
treading gingerly among bone artifacts
of shame and pride in the cerebral cortex
and limbic brain from bad poems committed
to the occasionally metric universe
and sometimes lost in the Mexican desert
I reach out my hand to her –

ARCHILOCHOS

Archilochos the soldier,
defeated in battle and running away,
has to leave his shield behind
on the battlefield:

"Well, what if some savage Thracian
finds the shield I had to abandon?
That's too bad. But it saved my skin,
I'm alive. And hell, I'll buy a better one."

While Bakchylides, Simonides and Pindar
wined and dined in rich men's houses,
Archilochos, with sword and shield, a soldier
on the field of battle, courted the Muses.

He died nearly three thousand years ago,
in the sea-dancing Ionian islands
– he wrote all his life: how to bear a blow,
to love life and even live with dying –

When he was promised Lykambes' daughter
by her father, and then refused her,
Paros Island rang with his fury –
And Lykambes? Cursed by all the gods.

He wasn't Homer, he wasn't anybody famous;
He sang of the people next door;
his language was their language; he died in battle
(with a brand new shield). Living was honour
enough for him, with death on every hand.
Archilochos the soldier, he was us.

Three thousand years? I can still hear
that commonsense song of the shield:
a loser who managed to be victorious,
his name is a champagne cry in my blood.

MAN WITHOUT A COUNTRY

An eagle does not know who he is
nor yet a rat nor lice in a dog's fur
none of them know who they are
in the speechless scream and snarl of being
And yet in a dark hole in earth rat is rat
louse biting blood from flesh is louse of lice
and in the eagle's scream is the whole sum
and mystery of being one of a flying nation
of birds in darkness in blood and riding
the shining helm of the sky...

But I have heard a man say
                    "This is not a country
                              I am going away from here"
It was as if he had said
                    "I am no man because –
                              because this is not a country"
– his face twisted in contempt for himself
and he spoke of all the great things
other countries had accomplished
one country in particular he named
and said "Look at them
their pride their arts and science
and above all they have not sold out
to the highest bidder
                              No I will not stay
I am no man here
because this is not a country"
and the loss was his overwhelming in sadness

I can see him now in my mind
going to and fro in the world
hobbling around on a one-legged syllogism

crying out to himself "I have no country!"
a warcry against himself
with nothing inside him except bitterness
and a condemnation of the place he came from
because he was not a man
because his country was not a country

Well let him be
for I have wondered who I was myself
as a youngster riding freight trains westward
noticing how the landscape in giant steps rose
to exceed itself in a continental hubris
of snow peaks and clouds piled skyward
with the hurtling upward roller coaster down sensation
that races thru blood with the alcohol of knowing
when dawn is the petals of a million flowers
with engine grit in my teeth and eyes stinging
with half the flying landscape a mince pie stuck to my face
the rest an omelet in shirt and pants and brain and under my
        fingernails
Call it inoculation – but not immunity
there is no immunity for place and time
and something grows inside if you feel it
and something dies if you don't
an exaltation
when I knew if anyone could ever know
what must escape telling and become feeling alone

I am a child fishing for sunfish in a river
I am learning to skate under the town bridge in Trenton
I am lost for two days in the northern forest
I am going to school and failing at French and Latin
I am learning what a strange lonely place is myself
reflecting the present reiterating the past
                    reconnoitring the future

These are my history
the story of myself

for I am the land
and the land has become me

Years later I think of that wandering exile
– and being an exile is beginning to understand yourself
as he is beginning to know that history is asleep
in all our bones the long history of becoming
He is beginning to know that the ruined grey cities
of Europe and eastern lands and ingrown culture
of the world mean nothing without a sense of place
the knowledge of here which is the centre of all things
of being a boy fishing for sunfish in a river
and always forever after knowing the direction of home
of things that resist telling the gods coded deep in memory
arriving here in total where the sun stands still at noon

Yes if you would like to hear his name said aloud
the name of the man without a country
for whom I feel such insulting compassion
that he would hate me for it if he knew
I can say that name but it would mean little
and perhaps he does know
and this poem of sadness and exaltation is written for him
tho poems speak names which are only words
and what words *are* there that you have not said yourself
which we must always go beyond
and arrive there naked
as it was in the beginning

THE INVISIBLE KIMONO

She wore a silk kimono
this young Japanese girl
in the Hiroshima peace park
– but didn't so much wear it
as lived in it like a landscape
a landscape of birds flowers trees
trees with that odd Japanese look
a look as if God had transplanted them
transplanted and made every tree different
different as people ought to be
so that trees were able to speak to you
tree-language bird-language flower-language
speak to you as if they sang the world to sleep
every night they sang the world to sleep
Finally it seemed to me that everyone
every Japanese girl everywhere
was wearing a silk kimono
even if it was invisible

Anyway I bought one
bought one for a girl in Canada
as near to the original kimono as possible
and imagined her inside it like a parade
down the main street of Belleville
while motorists honked enthusiastically
and Cadillacs courted Chevrolets
and sang Madame Butterfly to pedestrians
But it was no use – the kimono I mean
– she never wore it
couldn't figure out how to get inside
The hooks & loops & ties & things
spoke only Japanese not Canadian
However there was no disappointment
for somehow she is still wearing it

living in that landscape of trees and birds
birds like flowers that sing the world to sleep
every night they say their names to her
the trees & birds & grass & flowers
they say remember remember
as the thought of summer is more than summer
as love is larger than the tangible human body
tho each is impossible without the other
unless wearing the invisible kimono

ABC of P

Whoever wrote "Tom O'Bedlam,"
the anonymous, the all-of-us,
enduring the pain of everyman,
perched on a throne in the gutter.

Auden for "Lay Your Sleeping – " etcetera,
who was nevertheless anti-romantic;
a nay-saying man, a quiet torturer,
no spontaneity, decidedly magnificent.

Blake – who knew life's central things:
God, money (glory/power) and love.
Nobody can have all three of them:
Blake made two more than enough.

Byron for "So We'll Go No More – "
the glory of loss, the triumph of sorrow,
at Marathon, at Missolonghi:
no excuse given, none needed.

You, Gaius Valerius Catullus
" – here face down beneath the sun":
an absent friend, lost in the centuries' dust
next door, just stepped out for a minute –

Donne, of course, Dean of St. Paul's.
Just the early stuff. That death portrait,
sitting in his shroud, repels me:
the godless lover is alive and warm.

Homer and his characters struggle for control
in the ancient world of Achilles and Hector,
while Cassandra prophesies bloody hell –

You have to remind yourself now and then
this is literature.

Housman: aware of a moment coming
when human face and death's skullface
stare directly at each other,
and listened to what they said beforehand.

Jeffers, who was America's Cassandra.
I don't think he ever wrote of flowers,
but glimpsed another reality: dams broken
high in the mountains; after the bombers,
animals returned; earth grown bright –

Keats, the rejected – but rejection wasn't
so bad when you could soar like he did:
with a sadness so unbelievably poignant,
it escapes books and becomes gladness.

Kipling – still unfashionable:
for certain poems that awake the feeling
of woodsmoke in a simpler world,
and whatever poems do that prose can't.

Lawrence! – not for his blustering
Jesus-propheteering: just some delicacy
that stands on one foot and blushes
like a girl, then sticks out its tongue.

A yea-nay-sayer, the political Neruda,
who loved a mythic America
that never was –: in the blue distance
of Machu Picchu, and condors hovering.

Dylan and his childhood Forest of Arden,
whose life paraphrased his death:

as if there were artificial boundaries
between them, with booze in both places.

Yeats for Maud Gonne,
and those little glittering gay eyes
of the Chinese man: and because of him,
a feeling that greatness still lives.

Star painters, lapidaries, and often
poseurs; craftsmen more than artists;
but sometimes, when we had forgotten,
they remembered where the heart is.

UNFINISHED PORTRAIT

A really selfish face?
What nonsense!

Shadows under the eyes;
not big ones,
the kind a bird would make
if he accidentally stumbled
on a dust mote
between her and the sun,
ruining his high notes.
No, not selfish,
self-absorbed, I guess.
After all, is a squirrel selfish
because it likes nuts,
or an electron lyrical
from vitamin deficiency?
List imperfections,
not important ones tho,
conferring a shining:
too damn thin,
complexion superficially
imperfect – which
again is nonsense,
male nonsense.
What then?
On her face the look
of someone leaning
outward from a window
in spring and sticky buds
closing, unclosing, saying
"It's summer!"
or maybe spring:
but not saying it,

just thinking.
The look
between before and after,
when something is there,
and then isn't:
maybe that bird
mentioned earlier,
recovering
and vanishing –

AT LENIN'S TOMB

I'm part of the two-kilometre-long line-up
waiting to get into the mausoleum
– soldiers and shopkeepers and farmboys
fresh from the breadbasket Ukraine
in fact from all across the Soviet Union
shepherded by not-so-secret police
And this will be absolutely the first time
I have ever viewed any of the world's great corpses
For instance I have never seen Pasteur of Paris
Galen the Greek who lived in Rome
the American Salk (oops – pardon – he's alive)
Banting & Best of Toronto Schweitzer of Africa
those corpses have thus far evaded my eager gaze
In dim light we file past the glowing coffin
containing a very pale corpse with sandy goatee
and maybe it's a trick of the lighting
but do I notice a cobweb crawling from Lenin's ear
to his nose? Nonsense – such bad coffinkeeping
would not be permitted after the Revolution
Back home I look into an encyclopedia
adding a few more great corpses to the list
Klebs Harvey Koch Fleming Lister Ehrlich
and it's unlikely most of the crowd in Red Square
has heard those names and I admit I haven't
but I'm unable to handle gods and greatness
– psychologically speaking – and thus remains
in my mind the pale corpse of Vladimir Lenin
which actual as it is must still be considered
as only one small part of the total
and in no way invalidates those others

Moscow & Ameliasburgh

CAPITALISTIC ATTITUDES

"Gus" I said to Gustafson
"here in Russki land you indited
nineteen pomes I writ only eleven
Let us be true prosodic comrades
let us balance this disproportion:
I'll trade you one of mine
for five of yours
that oughta be a fair trade besides
I am well-known for my generosity"
Gus looks a mite peculiar
then turns me down flat
I can't understand it
I mean his selfish attitude

"Gus" I said as we stood
in Red Square on sore feet waiting
weeks to get inside Lenin's tomb
and St. Basil's candy-coloured spires
dreaming among the nightmare guns
"Gus" I said "if I trade my eleven
pomes for three by Pasternak
a sprig of orange mountain ash
from his house at Peredelkino
and the Boris troika for one by
Mayakovsky or two by Pushkin
and swap those to Voznesensky
along with Tretiak's good goal stick
and a puck to Voz for his pomes
on Oza and Mayakovsky's Typist
and I give you these in exchange
plus a quarter-full litre of vodka
do I get the okay for your nineteen?"

("Take your hands outa your pockets
capitalistic swine"

the Russki guard ordered
near Lenin's tomb and I did so)

Well it was a good try anyhow
The barter system does work sometimes
I figure even here in Russki land
it's share and share alike besides
approaching Pasternak Pushkin Mayakovsky
and Voznesensky's Oza with a proposition
like this for my mutual betterment
is as close to greatness as I'm likely
to reach given my modest abilities
And Lenin
when we shuffled past his tomb
as if all us serfs were wearing leg irons
pale Vladimir had nothing to say
which I took to be silent agreement
but now considering my increased total
of pomes I should approach Blok's "The Twelve"
"How about it Gus?"

Moscow

THE BLUE CITY

Of such an intense azure
that it seeps into your bones
providing dull earth
with an upsidedown sky
My wife is still sleeping
tired from the long journey
I have awakened very early
and must let her sleep longer
Her face is turned to one wall
of the strange hotel room
not feeling my own excitement
at being here with blood thrumming
and pulse beating a little faster
at the sheer romance of Asia
She turns over and sighs
while I'm standing at the window
trying to glimpse a camel
outside on awakening streets:
a woman is sweeping cobblestones
with some kind of twig broom
charcoal burning in a brazier
much blue ceramic but no camels
It occurs to me that I will remember
this time for its inbetweenness
removed from the continuity of things
and it's as if I'm a long way off
somewhere else and watching myself
watching a woman in bed sleeping
seeing what I see for the second time
the wished-for camel and burning charcoal
a blue city slowly coming awake
the little pulse in my wife's throat
I will be seeing it a second time
or has that second time arrived?

– My wife awakening not exactly
here nor there and aware of oddness
disoriented she keeps looking at me
brown eyes puzzled for a long moment

Samarcand & Ameliasburgh

ELEANOR AND VALENTINA

Tashkent girls are beautiful
a flat statement of fact
– Eleanor the Tatar guide
with high mythological
cheekbones is a case in point
She asks me about poems
and praises Soviet progress
I praise Eleanor
Samarcand girls are beautiful
that too is beyond dispute
is only a matter of degree
pertaining to an absolute
Valentina in Samarcand
dancing last night
and praises Soviet progress
she too is curious
about my poems
I tell them both
poems are about Valentina
poems are about Eleanor
the sweetness of honey
beyond the reach of bees
They smile like Bibi
Khanum and her architect
talk about Soviet progress
Valentina have I
made any progress?
Eleanor here's a poem
for you and I will intercede
with the city fathers
so that Tatar tribesmen
with horse-tail banners
may ride the steppes again
and you lead them

into Tamerlane's tomb
to intercede with death
and praise sex and life
while you extol again
Soviet progress
Here's our new theatre
Cotton is the principal export
Eleanor and Valentina I
will export you instead
your foreign exchange
will sunder the principalities
of heaven with red lips
on the stock exchange
and you will level
government buildings with
a mere tempestuous whisper
we will hop and step
and jump among the melons
we will declare
a moratorium on progress
we will eat grapes and
shishkabob in Samarcand
market and spit out
the seeds on
the mayor's new shoes
Valentina and Eleanor of
the lovely red lips
we will retrogress
forever in reverse
which is true progress
in search of absolutes
and I will hold both your
hands alternating currents
with grapes and pomegranates
while farmwagon mules
and market women marvel
and one grave dignified
old Uzbek tribesman

sings a sad little song
of wonder this morning
to Eleanor and Valentina
on the steppes of Central Asia

Samarcand

INTERNATIONAL INCIDENT

The market a riot of melons pomegranates grapes
Uzbek farmers selling fruit and their life times
– a mule cart loading cotton and melons
Tamerlane's tomb jade-blue and sky-blue mosaic
one step away from Bibi Khanum's own colour orgy
– ourselves the foreigners plain damn thirsty
me noticing this 8-year-old kid slurping ice cream
I point to it and raise my eyebrows questioningly
like *Where'd you buy the ice cream Kid?*
At that moment my bare arm is seized ungently
I am propelled away from the youngster
by an Uzbek with eyes like red-hot ball bearings
an ex-tribesman once one of Tamerlane's boys
now full citizen of Samarcand
"What gives?" I enquire in lordly fashion
knowing he can't understand a word of me
Our guide interrupts most fortunately
before my brains get scattered among the melon seeds
"He thinks you intend to photograph his wife and kid"
Well now I didn't even know he had a wife
and I don't possess a camera anyway
but thinking if I had photographed
this no doubt mysteriously veiled Asiatic beauty
some small hinder part would then have belonged to me?
– removed forthwith from her tribesmen and steppes
where they drink fermented ass's milk of nights
in felt yurts fingering their swords hoping
to be insulted and then take appropriate action
and the dancing girls trip over white men's skulls

Timur the Limper danced on my grave a brief moment
my skull considered a possible cornerstone for his pyramid
of skulls on accounta some no doubt grievous wrong
consummated on the blood descendant of Princess Bibi

– if not Timur why then an Uzbek mad as a hornet?
Possibilities are endless – in any case
I'm pleased family solidarity still has priority
even here on the steppes of Central Asia

Samarcand

And Timur again set out for the wars –
At this time (late 14th century),
there was not one man in the known world,
from high Pamirs to the Tien Shan Mountains,
who could say his name without trembling.
Timur then was deep in middle-age,
and looked it;
one foot had been lame from birth;
he wore a drooping Mongolian moustache;
no woman would call him handsome.
It may be that power is attractive,
and certainly fear is a factor,
and it may be that age has compensations:
in any event Bibi Khanum loved him.
The Chinese princess watched him go
(beautiful as a roomful of rainbows)
from the blue city of Samarcand:
a long dusty confused line
of horsemen and baggage animals
straggled toward the mountain passes,
short chunky men with faces like boards,
with oxhide shields and bone crossbows
and a leader who would conquer the world.

In 1977,
in the blue city of Samarcand,
a great stone sarcophagus
where Timur is said to be entombed,
waiting to leap out and conquer some more;
red and yellow portraits of Lenin
and Marx cover walls of buildings,
with the inevitable hammer and sickle,
while fleas hop from dust to dust mote.
Stand in a parking lot,

you can see shuddering heat waves
lift and dance across the steppes,
and more distant still the Tien Shan
Mountains and peaks of the high Pamirs,
where armies died of frostbite.
Nothing you can say or think
means very much:
you stand in a sort of trance
for several minutes,
until the dream-movements of a woman,
hanging out washing in the trembling sun,
shatter colour in your unfocussed eye,
domestic as dirt.
And thinking: in all this unwashed savagery,
thank god for women.

Samarcand

FOR EURITHE

I believe in death
the atoms of our bodies scattered forever
on the garbage dump of time

However
it is not unreasonable
that certain qualities of yours
– a constancy of the moon's orbit say
in relation to which I am an erratic
and undependable sun
strength like the bending branch
of some flowering tree
that intends to keep on doing it
a thereness and a nowness
definite as the orange flash
of an oriole between drops of rain
or the trailing yellow light
which marks a goldfinch passage
(I will not list the remainder
of ingredients like a chemist
on an aspirin bottle)

              – it is not unreasonable I say
that these qualities may
continue to exist and come
together again in the body of
one woman sometime in the future
(orange thereness of the oriole
yellow nowness of the goldfinch
brown sparrow at the sky's doorstep)
and they will attract people like me
(howlers at the moon)
whatever I pretend to feel
however I disguise myself

and someone very like you
and someone very like me
may exist at some unprovable time
on some unidentifiable star
sitting on the sun porch
trying to remember
something important

FATS SPEAKS
of love and marriage and life –

"I hung around in saloons
ever since I was two years old.
Sweets is the best thing
you can put in your body,
that's why I can play poker
five days and five nights.
I drink Cokes till they
come out of my ears.
French pastries I used to
eat 24 hours a day.
I do whatever I like
whenever I like.
If I had to do it again,
the only thing I wouldn't
do is get married."

FATS' WIFE, EVELYN
also has a few comments –

"Minnesota Fats is the most
vile, rotten man in the world.
I been married to this man,
come May 7, for 43 years.
He gets more vile every
day of his life. At home,
nothing but filth comes out
of his mouth. He definitely needs
to be prayed over. I don't
mind if you put this in the paper:
if Jesus got to him, He got
to him just in time to
save his rotten soul."

Found in Toronto *Globe & Mail,* May 5, 1984

TIME PAST/TIME NOW

Fathers, mothers: they were poor,
serfs on a great man's estate,
herdsmen on cropped bare hills,
maids at a lady's table.
Indentured all their lives,
chained by their souls to desks;
head down they plodded on,
in the track of someone else.

Cellar and hut and cave,
barn and shed and byre,
sullen they shovelled manure,
surly they lowered their eyes
when some great lord went by:
what a man was living for
was space to stand up straight,
two pennies made a fortune.

But there must have been once at least
some great blaze in their lives
– what other reason for living
but new feelings so unexpected
a man was puzzled in his mind
trying to figure it out?
– a woman half lost in a trance,
getting used to another self.

What could it have been? – not booze,
sex, mundane reward for virtue;
and maybe different for everyone,
the mystery that makes us human,
whatever "human" is –
– then blue aftermath and depression,

ever oncoming whips of trivia
to settle ourselves in dullness.

Coming alive at the womb's doorway,
we inherited everything – sun, moon,
all: and resent knowing more than we know,
the dictatorship of the senses enough,
the stone ship we ride on enough
for now – : then the rare arrival
of something entirely beyond us,
beyond this repeated daily dying,
the singing moment –

GONDWANALAND

(Some 200 million years ago – according to geological theory – there was only one landmass on earth, the supercontinent called Pangaea, meaning "single land." Then a large chunk broke away from Pangaea; it has been named Gondwanaland. The new Gondwanaland split up and drifted south and west to become Africa, Australia and South America. The remaining continent, now called Laurasia, also broke apart, some of it drifting west to become North America, the remainder Europe and Asia.)

The planet's basic stone
and what they did with it
those old ones:
– stone as art forms
shaped rearranged caressed worshipped
unknown men hammering stone on stone
common stuff from deep within
                                        earth's mantle
at Machu Picchu Sacsahuayman Carnac
artisans of the finite

Earlier still
stone islands grating against stone islands
(Gondwanaland dear lost Gondwanaland
and the worm's birthplace Pangaea
when one world self became many
and earth said to earth Goodbye)
when the birds the coloured birds
cried in their sleep for home
and dinosaurs riding stone galleons westward
an inch a year for centuries
lived and died like sailors

And stone as exterior decoration
sliced naked thru road cuts

of the Appalachians
and Precambrian Shield
grey oatmeal-porridge stuff
criss-cross tweedy patterns
stone like pink cooked ham
– or diamond speckled bits of light
twinkling on a party dress
across the millennia
in a bring-the-jubilee summons
to a five-billion-year-old
birthday on a one-room planet

(and perhaps two lovers –
their identity doesn't matter
– but maybe you and I are
those puppets caught up
in earth's divine passion
or mere human rut
hands linked in consecration
eyes trustful of each other
that the spell will last forever
– we join the celebration
while time performs its wonders
its carbon miracles)

Sedimentry rock
where a fallen leaf
prints itself on stone
and dies forever
Organic limestone
when skeletons of marine creatures
drifted down floating down in green gloom
each one turning a little in the water
and seeming to nod to each other
as they passed by
until their bones jostled in tiny mimic strugglings
with other bones at the misty graveyard
on the sea bottom

And fossil stone
in which mineral salts
have replaced animal bones:
far in the future a crew of
skeletons replacing living men
under earth's dying sun
crews of fossil mariners
riding ships of floating stone
without meaning or purpose
for there was never any purpose
and there was never any meaning –

Only that we listened to the birds
or saw how the sun coloured the sky
and were thoughtful in quiet moments
Sometimes in these short lives
when our minds drifted off alone
moving in the space vacated by leaves
to allow sunlight to pass thru
at the wind's soft prompting
there was reasonable content
that we were aware of only afterwards
and clapping our hands together like children
we broke the spell

Cairn on an arctic island
blind shape turned seaward
what sails rise there?

VICTORIA, B.C.

In a depressed blue mood
the day rain-grey
sky nearly weeping
then seeing masses of rhododendrons
a scarlet jubilee in the blood
the flowers half in startled air
and half their petals fallen
– even the ground is cheered up

Dec. 1929 to Feb. 6, 1930:
Beau Soleil villa, Bandol, France.
A field of yellow narcissus nearby,
blue glints from the distant sea.
A marmalade cat called Mickey,
for whom Lawrence pretended to be a mouse.
Frieda: "Lawrence was such a convincing mouse!"
Mme. Douillet's mother brought two goldfish,
"Pour amuser Monsieur."
They prospered while Lawrence coughed,
spitting his life into porcelain bowls –
Frieda: "Everything flourishes, plants
and cat and goldfish, why can't you?"
Lawrence: "I want to, I want to,
I wish I could – "
The worst time, just before dawn,
in false dawn fits of coughing.
He had said to her, "Come when the sun
rises." She came every day.
The English medico, Dr. Morland, gave
orders: he must not work, read,
have visitors. Visitors: Pino
Orioli, his publisher from Florence;
Norman Douglas, author of *South Wind*.
Earl Brewster, the American painter
friend, who had accompanied Lawrence
to the Etruscan tombs,
massaged his body every morning
with coconut oil: at this time,
his weight 6 stone (84 pounds).
And he worked with Frieda
on a wool embroidery design,
in chain stitch – probably using
old fashioned wooden crochet

hooks – : an old Etruscan peasant
with a white beard, dancing,
stepping light among spring flowers,
in time to some invisible flute,
his balls jiggling thru eternity;
a blue duck near the old man's head,
a saucy gold-coloured duck
prancing off on duck errands.
And all this time, the letters,
by train, boat, bicycle, horseback,
criss-crossing on the jet streams,
circling the world –
Feb. 6, 1930: Moved from Beau Soleil
to a TB sanitorium called
Ad Astra in Vence (from sun to stars).
The building resembling a resort hotel
in photograph: stucco, wide balconies,
flat roof with two gable promontories,
on which fancy decorative designs
– sun and full moon perhaps?
Lawrence's room with blue walls and
yellow curtains, a Mediterranean view.
Letter to Maria Huxley:
"I am rather worse here.
It's not a good place
– shan't stay long.
When do you think of coming?"
Work on a review of Eric
Gill's *Art Nonsense,* which
interested him. Frieda:
"Then he got tired of writing,
I persuaded him not to go on."
Sculptor Jo Davidson "made a clay
head of me – made me tired."
Visitors: H. G. Wells, the Aga Khan
("I liked him").
Friends arriving, Aldous
and Maria Huxley, Earl and

Achsah Brewster already there.
Frieda sleeping in a cane chair
in the blue room with yellow curtains,
waking to hear Lorenzo cough,
thin blood spattering,
staining his lips in darkness, a chill
wind veering in from the Mediterranean.
Dr. Morland: "I do not think much
of French sanitoria. He does not
seem to be responding to treatment."
Mar. 1, 1930: moved from Ad Astra
to Villa Robermond in Vence,
in a "shaking taxi" bouncing passengers.
Frieda at bedside, singing to him,
old songs they had often sung together.
Mar. 2 (Sunday), DHL to Frieda:
"Don't leave me, don't go away."
After lunch: "I have a temperature,
I am delirious. Give me the thermometer."
Frieda: "I cried, and he said 'Don't cry!'
Then he said, 'Hold me, hold me,
I don't know where I am,
I don't know where my hands are
– where am I?'"
Doctor injects morphine.
Lawrence: "I am better now, if only
I could sweat, I would be better –
I am better now – "
Frieda: "I held his left ankle
from time to time, it felt so full
of life, all my days I shall
hold his ankle in my hand – "
Shortly thereafter: gaps in breathing.
Breathing stops. The informing principle
absent. Slippers beside the bed,
formed in the shape of living feet.

"For me, the vast marvel is to be

alive. For man, or for flowers or
beast and bird, the supreme triumph
is to be most vividly and perfectly
alive. Whatever the unborn and the dead
may know, they cannot know the beauty,
the marvel of being alive in the flesh.
The dead may look after the afterwards.
But the magnificent here and now of
life in the flesh is ours, and ours alone,
and ours only for a time.
I am part of the sun as my eye
is part of me. That I am part of the earth
my feet know perfectly, and my blood
is part of the sea – "

DHL

LAWRENCE'S PICTURES

He is in all of them
some element of him
and so is Frieda
– turn your head away
from that stopped "Flight
Back Into Paradise"
and you know there's a
frenzy of action you can't see:
meanwhile back in Eden
Lorenzo is doing the dishes
Frieda watching
they yammer at each other
then start laughing
and pelt Jehovah with rotten apples
At the Feast of the Radishes
in Mexico enormous carved radishes
with red vegetable erections
seem to dominate
but weird white eyes peer
from under male sombreros
lost in their own darkness
and the red-bearded man
who is Lawrence
sitting while the others stand
a motionless centre
Only two lovers in the picture
in their rapt expressions
the red manikins disappear
They are a shining tremble
inside the still caught calm
and do not notice Lawrence
– pouring from their eyes
tiny replicas of themselves
In "Resurrection" Lawrence

is Christ turning toward Frieda
and life from the claws of Mabel Luhan
the nail holes in his hands
are healed but still death
lives in his empty eyes
Turn your own eyes away
and you see two white figures
running down a white road
into white distance
far from the rotting Cross
In "Rape of the Sabine Women"
which Lawrence also called
"A Study of Arses"
it is the furor of motion
writhing marble motion
a reverse William Blakeishness
that remains most prominent
the actual rape
is happening elsewhere
under the luminous bodies
And again Lawrence
or some element of him
turns away from the scene
"sex-in-the-head" abandoned
The man Christ-Lawrence
his hand on the woman's breast
she with her hand over his
in the "Holy Family"
a bemused child watching
unable to imagine feeling
the same way and unknowing
it will come to pass
The shepherd in "Boccaccio Story"
fallen asleep with penis exposed
the timorous nuns with balloon skirts
middle-aged and remotely young
who had forsworn such sights
passing in procession to watch

frightened yet attracted
by this pale glimmer of man
with no missing parts
a sun-bright devil
in their dark heaven

Nakedness in all these pictures
as if the stick figures
in Cro-Magnon cave paintings
suddenly achieved flesh
and the several million years
of yesterday when the human
race went forth unclothed
naked and without shame
had arrived again
whatever men and women had been
re-born
time reversed
and all the dead
with a kind of yearning
popping out naked from their graves
and the green world blossoming

MUSEUM PIECE

This boneyard of the dinosaurs
finds me footsore and tired
of all fleamarket history
that sets such store on paperclips
the toilet bric-a-brac of queens
their bowel movements chronicled
by scared astrologers
But ah the dinosaurs they soar
to fifteen twenty thirty metres
(or Biblical cubits if you prefer):
their body sounds of gurglings
rumblings of ancient indigestion
monstrous mooing love complaints
sunk to soft earthworm murmurs

Stand under these bone shadows
of tons of onetime flesh
and the mind harks back
to their heyday in the late
Cretaceous when the Great Death
came and saith: – "All life is mine"
– the red sun stopped its seeming flight
the planet's moon returned to night
when the shapeless shape no man hath seen
walked abroad in its shroud
and Eden gates went clang
shut with no sound

But ah they soared they Soar
this walled space makes no mock
of those with such enormous
appetites they ate the world
When museum cleaners come here
and leave aside their mops and brooms

to climb up teetery stepladders
with rags to wipe the weeklong dust
from fossil craniums they must
tremble a little no matter what
accident insurance rates are
The mind shuffles its feet to think
of that time: – when diplodocus tyrannosaurus
and the like trumpeted at the sky
65 million years ago
and it occurs to me that our human ancestors
then were small shrew-like creatures
hiding in holes probably nocturnal
– in that instant notice the cleaners
atop their stepladders have all changed
back into small shrew-like creatures
with tragic eyes

MY COUSIN DON

He fought his way up the Italian boot
with the Can. Army and diarrhea;
came home with something lost,
the "loss" remained with him always.

There are many things you lose
in a lifetime – family, friends,
the stubborn sense of who you are,
which is like living in an empty house.

We all know that "war is hell"
– it's been mentioned often enough;
but life generally flashes a signal,
some brief hint, the birth of something.

Of course:
there were dying men, mud and rain,
screams, cowardice, bravery,
prisoners shot, rape and desertion,
body and mind gone separate ways.

Back on the farm in apple orchards,
with a wife, who often must have said,
"It's over, all over"
– but the guns roared,
awake or asleep it never ended.

He left me one drunken night,
staggering, and I went to help him;
he turned with both fists ready to strike;
I bawled hell out of him for that.

I suppose what he lost, finally,
was trust in anything and everything,

including his wife, including me:
and cows shot guns, birds went bang.

Disaster is gradual like the seasons;
when star shells lighted his brain
I never knew: but his wife was gone,
his parents died; booze remained.

Disaster is also swift as a storm:
he had an affair with his best friend's wife:
she sat where train tracks crossed the farm,
when the train came she was cut in half.

– It was a Toonerville Trolley train,
it ran twice a week from the county seat,
it said "God is Love" on the morning milk run:
it killed her, and the gossip started.

Anyway, Don was thrown from his horse,
landed on his head and died later:
"He might better not have lived at all,"
his sister said, and "What was he alive for?"

Maybe she's right, but it's her opinion.
I remember the small boy:
he had grace, whatever grace is,
in an orchard in Prince Edward County

when we were children together,
and Macs, Spies, Tolman Sweets, Russets
– how they plopped rotten on earth,
with pigs crazy to get at them.

But the farm was acutely uncomfortable,
dank house, stern religious parents,
who made hell almost attractive,
and I kept going there again and again.

It was his grin – not cordial but real
– that greeted my visits: it said I'm Don,
I'm me – in that long-ago April
of the twin-conspirators against God.

I insist there was something, a thing of value.
It survived when death came calling
for my friend on an Italian battlefield:
not noble, not heroic, not beautiful –
It escapes my hammering mind,
eludes any deliberate seeking,
and all I can think of
            is apples apples apples . . . .

THE BOY ACCUSED OF STEALING

What have we to do with childhood?
– no one lives there any more
our replacements are small foreigners
or little dressed up dwarfs

Whenever I went back there
I had to build the buildings up
and recreate the sun and moon
the boy who stepped in every puddle

Sometimes the Airedale dog I loved
would growl to see me coming
this ghost stranger old dog time
he had no memory of

But it was worse to be ignored
although you knew you were real
but pinched yourself to make sure
and kept saying It's me It's me

My friend accused of stealing
I don't want to speak his name
for there would be shame to him
in my knowing what they were saying

I stand in the slightly amber air
of an old yellowing snapshot
which I hold in one hand
with a scratch on my finger

(I was always scratched and bruised)
and slowly another boy appears

out of the developing fluid
between my thumb and forefinger

– and the moment waited waited
and something emerged from our bodies
it stood between us quietly
a ghost that couldn't exist now

– the ghost of one & one are one
We stand among our desolations
which are like sorrows but worse
an exact foreknowledge of loss

a sorrow like death
except that the full electricity
of mile-wide frothing rivers
rages inside the hurt

(Good and evil will change places
many times in our lives
all the adjustable moralities
all the forgiveable selves)

We turned away finally
to go on being children
somewhere else a while longer
beyond Simmons' Drug Store

Now there are not quite duplicates
of ourselves standing where we stood
who never move and never speak
the shadows of old absolutes

FRIENDS

Whatever love is it includes them:
distant voices   metallic whispers
travelling words under sun and moon
over dark forests and blue water
reminder that you are human
and the pink jelly inside eggshell
skull dreams on a little longer

They have come to resemble the land
for me – perhaps in the same way birds
are shaped by thermal currents and wind
– my mind flashes to them
in bottom lands of mountain rivers
east central and maritime littoral
the prairies
fence posts on the unfenced plains
rich sediment of the Bearpaw Sea
glacial till that shaped their bones
soft clay and silt and yellow sand
with a mineral matrix
coalesced in the human flux

And having been alive here once
that is our signal to the future
the fragile jelly of our brain
is stained on time beyond removal
and the gods travelling into 1983
must encounter us and our friends
at this point if they wish to understand
what was always so hard for us
to comprehend: we are a few chemicals
that clotted together by accident
slowly becoming aware of our unimportance
Yet more than that: a bloodshot eye

set on a stone in a small galaxy
soon to wink out – with a ragged glory in its distorted vision

And the messages:
Yours sincerely
or insincerely as the
case may be
Your very truly
Yours respectfully
Yours until next time
Goodbye my dear
Au 'voir
With love
– With love?

AT MYCENAE

The dandelions
send up their white balloons
as they have since early time
over the high stone ruins
above the famous citadel
Perhaps a ploughman down below
stopped his horse in wonderment
and sighed a little
to watch the kings and queens go by
when the floating ghosts of flowers
scribbled birthmarks in the sky
in the hot still noon
their white balloons

Ploughmen of the dust
kings and queens at noon
who touched these walls
and their shadows too
dark parallels
the walls still exhale them
whose thoughts were stone
in the broken ruins

Below the citadel
a plain falls away
on earth so known to them
it must have seemed sometimes
that they could never leave
Lighter than air their thoughts
like small white balloons
touching stone and earth
and the floating clouds
anchored to this place
moored like the dandelions

to our drifting earth
where we cannot leave
and where we cannot stay
are stone and earth and clouds
and flesh for just a day

THE STRANGERS

It was nowhere that he came to,
away from a war with wife and children,
ox-drawn wagon, axe and rifle.
His thoughts went only two places,
where he had been, where he was now.
In a pine forest: trees so tall
weather was different at top and bottom.
His brain started to work on it
slowly: impossible to fell a whole
forest and burn slash before winter,
but perhaps enough for a garden patch?
How much sunlight does a man need? –
do crops need? – to achieve a sickly
yellow harvest, but still, to grow?
His eye swept the deep green ocean:
here a lean-to, on slightly higher ground,
built for shelter only, water nearby,
a permanent dwelling place later.
And something in him sighed at the thought
of permanence. Hefting the axe he ventured
among ancient giants – all far older
than himself, father and grandfather trees,
felling them a kind of patricide,
however necessary. Here a rotten trunk,
easy to bring down; one that *looks* weaker,
a hunch only – sliced waist high;
there a trunk the size of a man's body;
he blazed it for later; another selected
to join the condemned; and the rest girdled
for slow dying. And since the afternoon sun
was warmer, openings should point westward,
funnel-shaped, allowing light to fan out
among the stumps, shining on their death.
And then, maybe enough light

for rutabagas, potatoes and suchlike?
Maybe, maybe. Walking back through doomed pines,
where the wagon waited, a mourning wind
high overhead in topmost branches.
As much as possible in the green gloom,
he stepped from light to dark in criss-cross
shadows that were in no way ominous,
nor hinted at black and white winter.
Almost lighthearted, misgivings hidden
from himself, summer like a spell, the year
a war ended, happiness nearly impossible,
if such a thing was ever possible,
small content only now and then,
the wagon a wooden star ahead in his mind.
They waited, the youngest crying, his wife
making comforting sounds; oxen uneasy,
cropping sparse grass. Pale-haired woman,
her face scratched from underbrush,
thin from loss of nearly everything,
waited. Sons. Jed solid like his name,
an axe-handle boy. Philip a weak thing,
soon to die, he thought with sadness,
a premonition he hoped was wrong.
The girls unsmiling, impatient of course,
one with a white trillium on her dress,
much wilted now, picked along the way.
These were his entire world, here,
and felt tenderness in himself a weakness,
but forced a smile for them, thinking:
what strength there was, the tough fibre
of survival must reside in himself;
and Jed probably; perhaps his wife.
Her innards had not been well tested,
and would be now. Behind him the forest,
ahead the woman waiting, the crying child.

THE USES OF HISTORY

Leaving the dry library
and feeling a need for wetness
I settle myself in the Gatsby Lounge
at the nearby Quinte to partake same
and quaff a flagon or six
My books are laid out on the table
beside beer and ready for serious study
while strippers strip on-stage
and deafening music blares
This noisy cultural environment
does not inhibit my scholarly bent:
I read about the 16th century
Hindu kingdom of Vijayanagar
whose courtesans were so beautiful
that looking deeply into their eyes
caused some men to dance like raindrops
on water and others to howl like dogs
These girls were also "great
musicians, acrobats and dancers, very
quick and nimble in their performances"
Now a blonde stripper of outstanding
endowment explodes on centre stage
I gaze at her bemused but not unmoved
while other patrons watch raptly
and sip my beer in chosen solitude
not unlike Thoreau's at Walden Pond
until she dispenses with G-string
Returning to my studies: Mahommedan
raiders swoop down from the north and
besiege the little kingdom of Vijayanagar
the situation desperate whereupon
the king sends all his courtesans
to encourage his deprived army including
one Verynice whose attractions have come

down to us as six of the seven wonders
of antiquity and who was said to be
endlessly inventive and very expensive
beyond reach of bargain-hunters
Virtue of course triumphed
the Mahommedans fled leaving behind
their own considerable troupe of ladies
these inherited by Vijayanagar
and thought by certain sulky wives
to be much too much of a good thing
I am again distracted by events
beyond my control: a brunette stripper
similar to the Venus of Willendorf
springs on-stage with appropriate jiggles
as neo-classic music inspires her art
I note detachedly that her acrobatics
are quite beyond my own abilities
(other patrons go into shock
observing her prodigious measurements)
I abandon my books while Verynice
dances in several contrary directions
at once and I fear dislocations
in the space-time continuum as
femur and ulna tangle with my wishbone
mons veneris glows weirdly in a black
patch of light on-stage
and when she spreads her legs
standing on her devoted head
I can see thru the opening all
the way back to the 16th century
and into the little kingdom of Vijayanagar

A footnote to my scholarly treatise:
when Verynice died
(mourned by countless admirers)
she left a large fortune
some $100,000 in warm cash
(which in those days was a lotta bread)

including lingam and yoni to a favourite aunt
another slightly worn set as
surrogate to a bereaved customer

At the hotel desk after leaving
the Gatsby Lounge I overhear a now
fully dressed stripper and the manager
discussing financial arrangements and
I am struck by the tenderness in her
blue eyes as she contemplates the
timeless virtues of money
far beyond the borders
of the little kindgom of Vijayanagar

MACHINES

The Roll-edge

A hunchback shape
mounted on rails
with clacking jaws
into which you shoved
the mattress edge
with sharp ice pick
lifting it hard
while the needle stitched
a quarter inch distant
from my soft fingers
All day all day
walking backwards
continually pursued
but never quite caught
by a grey hunchback
that seemed to spit at you
becuse it was steel
and you were flesh

Nobody would teach me
how to run the thing
maybe they worried
they'd lose their own jobs
I practised at coffee break
punched out at noon
snuck back and studied it
the mystic machine
– and decided later
when I was able to think
calmly about it
that learning was like
wrestling someone
someone beyond me

enormously powerful
who could almost
casually
break my back
You could never win
the best to hope for
was not to lose
and $1.50 an hour

The Tufting Machine

A sliding table
also on rails
which held the mattress
You moved the table
to right then left
at spaced intervals
and a foot-long needle
popped buttons in fabric
like spaceships landing
My difficulty was rhythm
I didn't have it
a graceful hip-swing
precise but careless
like a boxer maybe
facing a hard puncher
the boxer with good left
sticking it in front of him
in the other guy's face
and the puncher's wild swings
just missing his chin
and he gets the decision
not really an award
but more personal

The reasons for doing it
learning the machines

never very clear
apart from money
However
an element of excitement
intermittent boredom
then the testing
a little tingle inside
and dubious splendour
You knew they watched you
workmen and foreman
emperor manager
their blank faces
meeting your blank face
carefully noncommittal
betraying nothing
for $1.50 an hour

The Filler

Quite uninteresting
and without problems
or scarcely any
demanding therefore
your ghostly minimum
and therefore allows you
to re-invent yourself
Besides the filler
was not elemental
like primitive roll-edge
which in a moment of
inattention could
break your bones
nor cerebral
like tufting machine
driving you crazy
but only the expected
fulfilling itself

Long after
it might be observed
by morticians or friends
that at a certain angle
the palm of my right hand
is slightly thickened
from using the ice pick
for those five years
a badge or memento
your average millionaire
would surely notice
of $1.50 an hour

CARPENTER'S NOTEBOOK ENTRY
(*Oct.* 14, 1891)

Builded a house last summer
for one William Knox
(Third Concession Ameliasburg Township)
the both of us having agreed aforetime
upon a fair reward for my labours
When the house was nearly builded
carved a unicorn with clasp knife
at one end of the gable roof
(the head only)
placed where it could not be seen
carved it from sweet resinous pine wood
that would soon mellow
and become a secret thing
I did not charge William Knox
(a choleric man of ill-temper)
for the extra time spent thereon
nor answer him uncivilly when
he shouted "Come down directly
from my rooftree Sir"

Years from now when we are
both no longer alive
after many seasons of rain
and many of shining
when the house returns to earth
the remains of my unicorn will
obey that long ago command
and lie in green grass
staring upward into the sky
with gold fur gold horn gold eyes
in the passion of dissolution

because I dreamed he will
and beyond his eyes my own
on land belonging to the heirs
and assigns of William Knox Esquire –

BIRDS HERE AND NOW

Always the gulls
white sails riding
high rivers of the sky
And one morning a dozen
robin clans at breakfast
on our green lawns
with bronze napkins
tucked under chins
heads cocked in wise looks
enquiring at my window
about human migration
"Why so far from home?"
Noisy starlings
jabbering together in
one-syllable language
aa-sounding only
unable to manage
our ghostly consonants
the little stammerers
at words' beginnings
Absurd pelicans
stand on streetcorners
which in this case
means docks and jetties
In the air they lose
any absurdity
– I think of flying
paintings I think
of heavy iron
sculpture become
weightless

Our bird visitors
most of them in

continual transit
voyageurs and sky
travellers elsewhere:
now is here and tomorrow's
country may be Asia
Patagonia Quintana Roo
place mixed together
with time – earthen-time
both see-throughable
the same
not the same
a jump of the mind
necessary
for flying
humanly impossible
sadly beyond us
– the bird's blue shadow racing
over the earth and our local
heartbeat matching its wingbeat
in Australia
tomorrow's Asia
yesterday's Europe
in the blood's imagination
only otherwise
flightless

STORY

Thirty years ago
they got married and had children
lived in a town beside the sea
and waves poured in across the sand
in hills beyond the town wind blowing
and sometimes white ships passed by
out at sea as if in someone else's dream

Whatever happiness may be it touched them
with the high seriousness of lovers
who know they are lucky from watching other people:
whose lives rise and fall in peaks and valleys
like the sea waves' constant rise and fall
elated at nothing much and then depressed
because the novelty wears off
and yesterday was just the same as tomorrow

Of course the lovers had that feeling too
since everyone is aware of it more or less
the desolation of vast wastes of time
the monotony of each action so similar
to the last it seems a continual rehearsal
for some great event that never happens
for which many of us get tired of waiting

But our lovers were more fortunate
because they loved or for other reasons
the high emotional peaks and troughs
of despair were levelled to a slight rise and fall
much like the motion of that white ship at sea
whereby no passenger was in any way aware
of underwater mountains and submarine disasters
reflected in their lives

Then they stopped being lucky
the woman ill with cancer
a terminal illness the disease deadly
whether she was aware of this or not
and probably she was
as others have been for thousands of years
whispering goodbye to whoever loved them

Here I intrude myself
to say this story was told me
by the man who was my friend
who saw how the cancer ate her life
and shrank her body down to half
while he kept his surface feelings under control

He slept upstairs and this one morning
in the story came downstairs
naked to visit his wife
naked because he slept that way
and because all of us are part of nature
came down with a large erection dangling
not really a sexual signal
but indication his equipment was in order
the woman seeing it smiled weakly and said
"Sorry love I can't do much about it"

That's most of the story
of course she died and was buried
and in a fairly short time my friend will die too
but it seems worthwhile mentioning all this
as something one would like to feel as well
– not the gruesome part but the tenderness
of someone before being swept out to sea
who says everything to you in a single phrase

The town they lived in is little different
white ships pass far away in sunlight
there are dances at night sometimes no doubt

and another young couple might lean against the rail
of one of those ships
to gulp fresh air and glance toward the land
where vague lights blur in darkness
wind sweeps over hills beyond the town
waves pour in across the sand
and the ship sails on –

THE SON OF SOMEONE LOVED –

If you loved an entire species
it would be similar but simpler
a kind of gooey peanut butter spread
enveloping all tortoises say
because their faces resembled Hebrew prophets
or all elephants because of phallic envy
or all hippos because they're so alien
to Venus emerging from her television bath
and gaze soulfully at herds of them in a zoo
But to love a single member
of any species is the special human lunacy
recipe for wars and nuclear disaster

In this case isolate
your own feelings of affection
for small endearing habits of hers
then transfer and split that affection
for a surrogate kid
– allowing say 10 points or 12
to him for each charming her-extract
add them all up like Gregor Mendel
divide and subtract the sum
with a computer in your head
and damn the nasturtiums

Tear a rainbow's spectrum apart
separate the moon into favourite phases
Beethoven's Fifth into set pieces
of vest-pocket melody
which examples go to prove
originals are not divisible
Include Breughel's Fall of Icarus
as exception
where such logic is umbilical

the boy drowns like a footnote
(notice also that uncanny turning away
from the event which Auden pointed out)
– while the inventor father Daedalus
returned to the laboratory at Knossos
is falling in love with his new mistress
the variable pitch propeller

The sun does not give birth to daughters
nor moon to other moons
– but Beethoven to Beethovens?
and Breughel to more Breughels?
Anyway it was a mistake
it happened in another country
of witches magicians satyrs undines
a negotiated settlement is contemplated

Here all is ordinary
but the mind-flash remains
sun at zenith moon at apogee
Beethoven Breughel the works
and morning the very early morning
when flowers open and birds begin to sing
a far country
where lawns are emerald
and from each blade of grass
drops of dew sparkle
that have not yet fallen
(This circumstance is recorded severally
in lieu of earth air fire water
– "formerly believed to constitute
all physical matter" –
but non-metaphysically
and certainly non-definitive chemically
somewhere between fire and earth
add one more)

MARVIN MOLLUSC

150 million years
ago a particular
fossil mollusc lived
and died in seas then
covering Scotland
Moreover he was born
in summer when water
temperature was 70 F.
lived four years
and died in springtime
However the fossil's love
life in his warm bath
number of times a night
in jurassic moonlight
and degree of enjoyment
from same remains
unknown

This information derives
from laboratory researches
of one Dr. Harold
Urey in Chicago
The unfortunate mollusc –
we shall call him Marvin
– had a chalky shell
whose special composition
was determined by degree
of water temperature
After various dating
devices were employed
on Marvin's mortal
remains (sophisticated
successors of Carbon-14)
and the figure 150

million arrived at
for his birth date
the shell was analyzed
(chemicals etcetera)
results of this invasion
of privacy published
in scientific journals

This special information
on the fate of Marvin
has caused me to alter
my views on disposition
of my own mortal
remains hopefully
at a much later date
I have therefore instructed
my heirs and assigns
that I be cremated
and furnace temperature
should reach several
thousand degrees
I am reluctant to leave
traces of my chalky
structure to fall into
the hands of Dr. Harold's
nosy descendants
especially the falling
temperature and certain other
details of my love life
I think my friend Marvin
would agree with
this point of view

DOG SONG 2

Sooner or later
it all comes thronging back
everything that ever happened to you:
suddenly I find myself singing
and I can't sing worth a damn
which doesn't matter anyway
standing on the stony shoreline
of an arctic island watching icebergs
drifting in white night of Cumberland Sound
like ghost ships of lost explorers
trying to find safe passage
thru the ice trying to get home
and without awareness of doing it
I began to hum deep in my throat
then burst out singing with voice cracking
from fever I'd just recovered from –
The actual song-words didn't matter
but for a moment I was prehistoric man
coming out of his cave at night to howl
from sheer self-importance
because he was a damn good hunter
or because a woman had smiled
And the song said: Hello my friends
Hello my friends because we're friends
let's have a drink while we're alive
And the song said: Let's have a drink
for no reason or any reason
and because there's a time in your life
like bacon frying like stars exploding
and you stand on your hind legs and sing
because you're a dreaming animal
trapped in a human body
After a while there was a little echo
the merest whine and whimper and thread

of sound when a sled dog joined me
then another and another
in solemn sadness with a great undertone
of exaltation from weary arctic miles
they had all travelled together
with balls of ice torturing their feet
and whips biting hairy shoulders
and starvation meals of frozen fish
so hard it was like eating fire
they sang the soul's grief of being trapped
and knowing it inside an animal's body
and the dogs mourned

We stopped and there was silence
but not an empty silence
Jonahsie and Leah stood in their doorway
watching me with a peculiar look
but I grinned at them
while the great floating ice castles
swayed by at the edge of the world –

THE TARAHUMARA WOMEN

West by train from Chihuahua
into dry Mexican mountain country
to Creél
                    land of the Tarahumaras
Indians so fleet of foot
they run down the running deer
and cause them to die from exhaustion
which isn't very attractive either
but likely mythical
Anyway there we are
my wife and myself
plus an American family of four
in a tourist panel truck from Creél
to visit the Tarahumaras

                              – in a cave
cold and smoky and high-vaulted
nature's slum cathedral
nothing like home-sweet-home
the campfire whispering softly
a bucket of maize bubbling
men somewhere else
three women and two kids
one washing her kid's face
and hands with dirty water
one tending the fire
another trying to sell little dolls
that were almost human

                    – I hadn't fully realized
(or so I plead to myself)
the difference in their lives from mine
the absence of pride
the absence of everything

except dirt
                – but I'm thankful
for I did not see in their faces
                that look of recognition
making each of us vulnerable to the other
that queer knowing
distinguishing us from other animals
there was just dull acceptance
from which I took no comfort
                when I ran away
                when I was ashamed
My wife had already gone
feeling what I did before I did
but instinctively
whereas I had to think about it
And now months later
troubled that I thought more of myself
and my reactions than I did of them
the Tarahumara women
still waiting to see their expressions
change into contempt
or at least anger
for the gringo who bought nothing
and paid for it

Mexico

CHOICES

Small shrines beside Mexican roads
tiny adobe chapels
or mere piles of stones
with artificial flowers sometimes
scissored from coloured plastic
surmounted by the inevitable cross:
where a farm labourer was struck by a car
where a poor paisano died
some ragged Jesus or dimpled Maria
and their relatives and loved ones
erected these small memorials
Above all they are not ostentatious
wealth has nothing to do with it
even a pyramid of six or seven stones
has the same meaning
as the slightly more elaborate adobe chapels
They mark the sadness and grief of being loved
loved so intensely it is like a flame
as if some clotted choked emotion
hovered tangible in air
even after blood is washed away in rain
which is all the living can give the dead
There are never any names
no indication of identity
but there is never any doubt of love
which is so commonplace and rare
that it must be genuine
as well as part of religious protocol
It makes me wonder about myself
and which should I prefer:
a poet's brief undying fame in words
or this love

that shrieks silently beside the highway?
But there is no choice possible
neither my little whispering words
entombed in books and magazines
nor the shrieking stones

Mexico

IN CABBAGETOWN

On cool nights I would creep
from the Cabbagetown house
on Sackville Street to Riverdale
Zoo with hard-beating heart
entering the monkey cage at 2
A.M. with an orange-bitten moon
over one shoulder and wondering:
"Why should the moon taste good
and to whom?"
"You you you"
sang the little primates "But
Quiet Quiet now
the zooman sleeps in his cage of wood
and the wallpaper stars shine thru"
Then they told me about Africa

After the drunks on Parliament Street
released from Winchester pub
like fleas fled fast to their beds
I came
to the mountain lion's house
in the high dry country of Colorado
at cloud-hung Nimpkish Lake
when the big firs sang the wind
to a silver slurp on Forbidden Plateau
he nuzzled his mother's hairy dugs
that glowed in the dark glowed in the dark
in his head
He said
"Tell me why
the red lights change to green at Queen
& Bay when there's no one about
– no one about?"

I couldn't say
but the zooman slept nearby
at Toronto Crematorium Brown
and Mackenzie slept their dead
thoughts stopped at 3 A.M.
At 3 A.M.
                the clocks struck Three
                         – Three they said three times

The woman in bed with shoulder bare
and one breast shone like a moon Mare
I left I came
                  to the elephant towns
and grey houses on four legs moved
houses the colour of earth rolled by
while Toronto slept and moaned in sleep
the great trunks held me close
And the herd bull said
                                   "Tell me of India
tell me of snakes and antelopes
the burning ghats where Ganges shines
I was born here and do not know
Speak about jungle heat
when the tiger's whiskers drip sweat
and the monsoon sighs in Cawnpore night
I can't forget I can't forget
what I have never known"
"Four Four Four Four"
said clocks somewhere

The zooman woke in policeman blue
pointing his sixgun finger at me
"Get Out Get Out" and I
fled back to bed on Sackville Street
in Colorado and Nimpkish Lake

and a wind-sung skein of moon
on the Forbidden Plateau lulled me to sleep
in India and Africa dreaming of
what I can't forget
dreams I have never known –

DOUG KAYE

Listening to Jussi Bjoerling's
opal diamond sapphire emerald voice
Doug materializes in the chair opposite
following the sunlit trajectories
into unicorn country
                                        and also hearing
Amor ti vieta traduce and libel
romance to his three wives
(or was it five?) and *E lucevan*
le stelle drowns with new melancholy
the old melancholy
of being alive

It was an excellence of some sort
his mind worked towards
that stayed just beyond his reach
(violin lessons a failure
marriages ending one by one)
the factory we both worked at
a hullaballoo of dissonance
so that most of what he was was
invisible and given over to silence

A tomahawk lodged in his brain
the pain soothed only by Bjoerling
Gigli Tebaldi Callas and bel canto
while another voice a hound voice
belled among the crashing machines
sending him backward to repeat the past
back to the point of entry
searching for a trapdoor to infinity
I remember
we punched out at noon one day
to eat lunch on grass

and thinking
of life being “nasty brutish and short”
I asked him why this search
and he said with sadness
“What else could I possibly do?”

IN THE EARLY CRETACEOUS

They came overnight
a hundred million years ago
the first flowers ever
a new thing under the sun
invented by plants
It must have been around 7 A.M.
when a shrew-like mammal stumbled
out of its dark burrow
and peered nearsightedly
at the first flower with
an expression close to amazement
and decided it wasn't dangerous

In the first few centuries later
flowers began to cover the earth
in springtime they glowed
with gleaming iridescence
not just a tiny bouquet
like the colours on a mallard's neck
before mallards existed
or like god's earmuffs
before Genesis was written
and even tho nobody was there
to analyze it
they nevertheless produced a feeling
you couldn't put a name to
which you could only share
like moonlight on running water
                    leaf-talk in the forest
the best things right under your nose
and belonging to everyone

And one of the early inhabitants
a comic-looking duck-billed dinosaur

might have lifted his head
with mouth full of dripping herbage
and muttered Great Scott
or something like it
Triceratops gulped a township
of yellow blossoms
diplodocus sampled blue
for several horizons
and thought it was heavenly
and colour became food

It was not a motionless glory
for colours leaped off the earth
they glowed in the sky
when wind blew great yellow fields
danced undulating in sunlight
hundreds of miles of blue flowers
were dark velvet in starlight
and maybe some unnamed creature
stayed awake all night in the
midst of a thousand miles of colour
just to see what it felt like
to have all the blue-purple there was
explode in his brain
and alter both present and future

But no one will ever know
what it was like
that first time on primordial earth
when bees went mad with pollen fever
and seeds flew away from home
on little drifting white parachutes
without a word to their parents
– no one can ever know
even when someone is given
the gift of a single rose
and behind that one rose
are the ancestors of all roses

and all flowers and all the springtimes
for a hundred million years
of summer and for a moment
in her eyes an echo
of the first tenderness

ACKNOWLEDGMENTS

The Beaver
Canadian Broadcasting Corporation
The Canadian Forum
Canadian Literature
The Moosehead Review
Poetry Australia
Poetry Canada Review
Prism International
Rampike
Saturday Night
Toronto Star
Queen's Quarterly
Waves

And seven poems from
two limited editions are included:
Birdwatching at the Equator and
Moths in the Iron Curtain.

With special thanks to the Canada Council and
the Ontario Arts Council.